Blastoff! Readers are carefully developed by literacy experts to build reading stamina and move students toward fluency by combining standards-based content with developmentally appropriate text.

 Level 1 provides the most support through repetition of high-frequency words, light text, predictable sentence patterns, and strong visual support.

 Level 2 offers early readers a bit more challenge through varied sentences, increased text load, and text-supportive special features.

 Level 3 advances early-fluent readers toward fluency through increased text load, less reliance on photos, advancing concepts, longer sentences, and more complex special features.

★ **Blastoff! Universe**

Reading Level

 Grade K

 Grades 1–3

 Grade 4

This edition first published in 2021 by Bellwether Media, Inc.

No part of this publication may be reproduced in whole or in part without written permission of the publisher. For information regarding permission, write to Bellwether Media, Inc., Attention: Permissions Department, 6012 Blue Circle Drive, Minnetonka, MN 55343.

Library of Congress Cataloging-in-Publication Data

Names: Mattern, Joanne, 1963- author.
Title: Hamburgers / by Joanne Mattern.
Description: Minneapolis, MN : Bellwether Media, Inc., 2021. | Series: Blastoff! Readers |
  Includes bibliographical references and index. | Audience: Ages 5-8 | Audience: Grades 2-3 |
  Summary: "Simple text and full-color photography introduce beginning readers to hamburgers.
  Developed by literacy experts for students in kindergarten through third grade"–Provided by publisher.
Identifiers: LCCN 2020036799 (print) | LCCN 2020036800 (ebook) | ISBN 9781644874356 |
  ISBN 9781648341120 (ebook)
Subjects: LCSH: Hamburgers--Juvenile literature.
Classification: LCC TX749.5.B43 M32 2021 (print) | LCC TX749.5.B43 (ebook) | DDC 641.6/62--dc23
LC record available at https://lccn.loc.gov/2020036799
LC ebook record available at https://lccn.loc.gov/2020036800

Text copyright © 2021 by Bellwether Media, Inc. BLASTOFF! READERS and associated logos are trademarks and/or registered trademarks of Bellwether Media, Inc.

Editor: Kieran Downs   Designer: Brittany McIntosh

Printed in the United States of America, North Mankato, MN.

Table of Contents

Good Taste on a Bun	4
Hamburger History	8
Hamburgers Today	14
Glossary	22
To Learn More	23
Index	24

Good Taste on a Bun

meat patty

grill

It is a warm summer day. You take a meat **patty** off the **grill**. Then you place the patty on a bun.

You take a bite! The burger is **seasoned** perfectly. Hamburgers are **delicious**!

Hamburgers are **ground beef** made into patties. You can cook them on a grill or in a pan. Then you place them on buns.

How to Make Hamburgers

1. Place a hamburger patty on a hot grill
2. Cook on both sides
3. Place the patty on a bun
4. Add toppings and enjoy!

You can add tasty toppings like ketchup and mustard. Hamburgers make a great meal!

Hamburger History

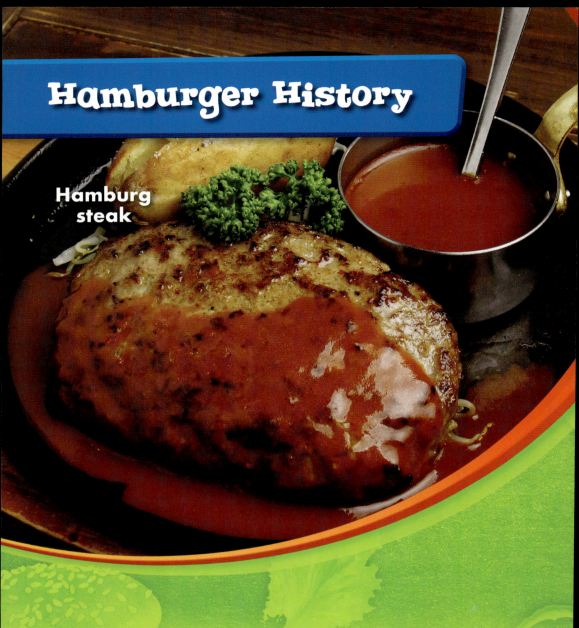

Hamburg steak

Hamburgers got their name from Hamburg, Germany. In the 1800s, people in Hamburg chopped up meat to make Hamburg steaks.

German **immigrants** brought the steaks with them to the United States.

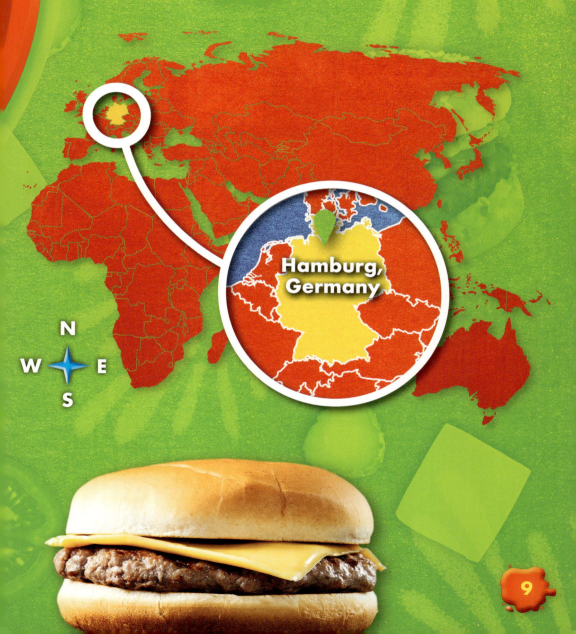

Easy Hamburgers

Ask an adult to help you make these tasty hamburgers!

Tools

- large frying pan or grill
- meat thermometer
- spatula

Ingredients

- 1 pound (0.5 kilograms) ground beef
- hamburger buns

Instructions

1. Heat up a grill or a pan on the stove.
2. Form the beef into four equal-sized patties.
3. Place the patties into the pan or on the grill. Be careful!
4. Cook the patties on each side for about 3 to 4 minutes or until the center of each burger is at least 160 degrees Fahrenheit (71 degrees Celsius).
5. Place burgers on buns and serve.

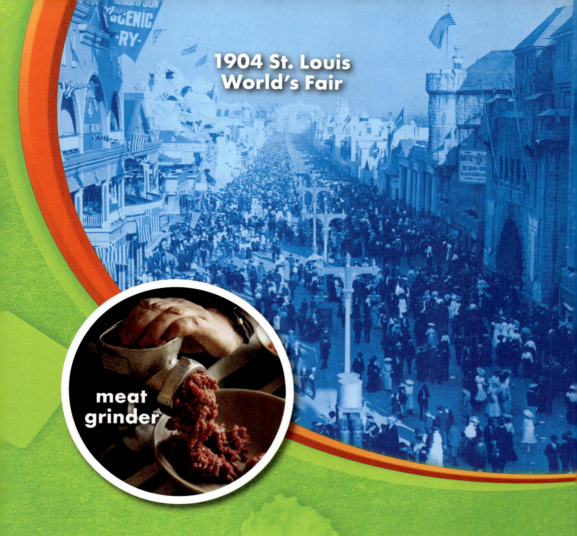

1904 St. Louis World's Fair

meat grinder

In the late 1800s, **meat grinders** became available for people to buy. The first hamburgers were created soon after. Hamburgers on buns became popular at the St. Louis World's Fair in 1904.

In 1921, White Castle opened its first restaurant in Kansas. Soon, other White Castles opened around the country. It became the first burger **chain**.

Hamburger Timeline

1800s
Hamburg steaks are eaten in Germany

1904
Hamburgers on a bun are popular at the St. Louis World's Fair

1921
The first hamburger restaurant, White Castle, opens

White Castle hamburger

McDonald's restaurant

Others followed. In 1948, the first McDonald's opened in California.

Hamburgers Today

Today, hamburgers are one of the most popular foods in the United States. Around 50 billion are eaten every year!

They can be found in both fast-food and fancy restaurants.

fast-food burger meal

hamburger toppings

Hamburgers can have different toppings. Cheese and bacon are popular.

Vegetables like lettuce, tomatoes, and pickles are all common. Different sauces add different flavors.

Tasty Toppings

There are many common topping combinations that make favorite hamburgers. Try these ones out!

cheeseburger
cheese

bacon cheeseburger
bacon + cheese

Hawaiian burger
pineapple

breakfast burger
fried egg

pizza burger
mozzarella cheese + tomato sauce

Hamburgers are made from ground beef. But other foods can be used to make burgers, too!

turkey burger

black bean burger

Some people like turkey burgers. Others make **vegetarian** burgers out of black beans or vegetables.

In 2017, the world's largest hamburger was made in Germany. It weighed 2,566 pounds (1,164 kilograms). What would you put on that hamburger?

Juicy Lucy

Have an adult help you make these burgers with cheese inside!

Tools

- large frying pan or grill
- spatula
- meat thermometer

Ingredients

- 1 pound (0.5 kilograms) ground beef
- 4 slices of cheese
- buns

Instructions

1. Heat a grill or a pan on the stove.
2. Form the beef into eight small, equal-sized patties.
3. Cut each slice of cheese into four small, equal-sized pieces.
4. Take a patty and place four small pieces of cheese in the center. Place a second patty on top of the cheese and seal the edges together.
5. Repeat step 4 three more times. You will have four patties filled with cheese.
6. Cook the patties on each side for about 3 to 4 minutes or until the center of each burger is at least 160 degrees Fahrenheit (71 degrees Celsius).
7. Place burgers onto buns. Be careful, the cheese inside will be very hot!

Glossary

chain—a set of different restaurants in different locations that share one owner

delicious—very tasty

grill—a metal frame used to cook food over a fire

ground beef—meat that comes from cows that has been cut into very small pieces

immigrants—people who move to another country

meat grinders—machines that chop up meat into very small pieces

patty—ground meat pressed into a small, flat cake

seasoned—covered in spices for flavor

vegetarian—made without meat

To Learn More

AT THE LIBRARY

Golkar, Golriz. *Hamburgers*. Minneapolis, Minn.: Pop!, 2019.

Kuskowski, Alex. *Cool Hamburger Recipes: Main Dishes for Beginning Chefs*. Minneapolis, Minn.: Checkerboard Library, 2017.

Mattern, Joanne. *French Fries*. Minneapolis, Minn.: Bellwether Media, 2020.

ON THE WEB

FACTSURFER

Factsurfer.com gives you a safe, fun way to find more information.

1. Go to www.factsurfer.com.

2. Enter "hamburgers" into the search box and click 🔍.

3. Select your book cover to see a list of related content.

Index

bun, 4, 6, 11
California, 13
chain, 12
Germany, 8, 9, 20
grill, 4, 6
ground beef, 6, 18
Hamburg, 8, 9
Hamburg steaks, 8, 9
history, 8, 9, 11, 12, 13, 20
how to make, 6
immigrants, 9
Kansas, 12
McDonald's, 13
meal, 7, 14
meat grinders, 11
pan, 6
patty, 4, 6
recipe, 10, 21
restaurant, 12, 14
sauces, 17
seasoned, 5
St. Louis World's Fair, 11
timeline, 12
toppings, 7, 16, 17
turkey burgers, 18, 19
United States, 9, 14
vegetarian burgers, 19
White Castle, 12, 13

The images in this book are reproduced through the courtesy of: Gena73, front cover; MaraZe, p. 3; LauriPatterson, p. 4; stockcreations, p. 5; Scruggelgreen, p. 6 (step 1); Wally Stemberger, p. 6 (step 2); DebbiSmirnoff, p. 6 (step 3); AnnaKalinicheva, p. 6 (step 4); witty234, p. 7; fumi901, p. 8; Drozhzhina Elena, pp. 9, 10; Renan Teuman / Alamy Stock Photo, p. 11 (top); Ganna Petrova, p. 11 (bottom); Drew Angerer / Staff / Getty Images, p. 13 (bottom); DPD ImageStock / Alamy Stock Photo, p. 13 (bottom); pancha.me, p. 14; New Africa, p. 15; UvGroup, p. 16; Michael Kraus, p. 16 (cheese slice); Sergiy Kuzmin, p. 16 (bacon); Alex Staroseltsev, p. 16 (pineapple); Dr.Margorius, p. 16 (egg); timquo, p. 16 (mozzarella); studiovin, p. 16 (tomato sauce); Brent Hofacker, pp. 18, 19; Happy cake Happy cafe, p. 20; ALEX S, p. 21.